I0409732

THE PRESIDENT'S VISIT TO VIETNAM: A MISSED OPPORTUNITY TO ADVANCE HUMAN RIGHTS

HEARING

BEFORE THE

SUBCOMMITTEE ON AFRICA, GLOBAL HEALTH, GLOBAL HUMAN RIGHTS, AND INTERNATIONAL ORGANIZATIONS

OF THE

COMMITTEE ON FOREIGN AFFAIRS
HOUSE OF REPRESENTATIVES

ONE HUNDRED FOURTEENTH CONGRESS

SECOND SESSION

JUNE 22, 2016

Serial No. 114–213

Printed for the use of the Committee on Foreign Affairs

Available via the World Wide Web: http://www.foreignaffairs.house.gov/ or
http://www.gpo.gov/fdsys/

U.S. GOVERNMENT PUBLISHING OFFICE

20–530PDF   WASHINGTON : 2016

For sale by the Superintendent of Documents, U.S. Government Publishing Office
Internet: bookstore.gpo.gov   Phone: toll free (866) 512–1800; DC area (202) 512–1800
Fax: (202) 512–2104   Mail: Stop IDCC, Washington, DC 20402–0001

COMMITTEE ON FOREIGN AFFAIRS

EDWARD R. ROYCE, California, *Chairman*

CHRISTOPHER H. SMITH, New Jersey
ILEANA ROS-LEHTINEN, Florida
DANA ROHRABACHER, California
STEVE CHABOT, Ohio
JOE WILSON, South Carolina
MICHAEL T. McCAUL, Texas
TED POE, Texas
MATT SALMON, Arizona
DARRELL E. ISSA, California
TOM MARINO, Pennsylvania
JEFF DUNCAN, South Carolina
MO BROOKS, Alabama
PAUL COOK, California
RANDY K. WEBER SR., Texas
SCOTT PERRY, Pennsylvania
RON DeSANTIS, Florida
MARK MEADOWS, North Carolina
TED S. YOHO, Florida
CURT CLAWSON, Florida
SCOTT DesJARLAIS, Tennessee
REID J. RIBBLE, Wisconsin
DAVID A. TROTT, Michigan
LEE M. ZELDIN, New York
DANIEL DONOVAN, New York

ELIOT L. ENGEL, New York
BRAD SHERMAN, California
GREGORY W. MEEKS, New York
ALBIO SIRES, New Jersey
GERALD E. CONNOLLY, Virginia
THEODORE E. DEUTCH, Florida
BRIAN HIGGINS, New York
KAREN BASS, California
WILLIAM KEATING, Massachusetts
DAVID CICILLINE, Rhode Island
ALAN GRAYSON, Florida
AMI BERA, California
ALAN S. LOWENTHAL, California
GRACE MENG, New York
LOIS FRANKEL, Florida
TULSI GABBARD, Hawaii
JOAQUIN CASTRO, Texas
ROBIN L. KELLY, Illinois
BRENDAN F. BOYLE, Pennsylvania

AMY PORTER, *Chief of Staff*   THOMAS SHEEHY, *Staff Director*
JASON STEINBAUM, *Democratic Staff Director*

––––––––

SUBCOMMITTEE ON AFRICA, GLOBAL HEALTH, GLOBAL HUMAN RIGHTS, AND INTERNATIONAL ORGANIZATIONS

CHRISTOPHER H. SMITH, New Jersey, *Chairman*

MARK MEADOWS, North Carolina
CURT CLAWSON, Florida
SCOTT DesJARLAIS, Tennessee
DANIEL DONOVAN, New York

KAREN BASS, California
DAVID CICILLINE, Rhode Island
AMI BERA, California

CONTENTS

THE PRESIDENT'S VISIT TO VIETNAM: A MISSED OPPORTUNITY TO ADVANCE HUMAN RIGHTS

WEDNESDAY, JUNE 22, 2016

House of Representatives,
Subcommittee on Africa, Global Health,
Global Human Rights, and International Organizations,
Committee on Foreign Affairs,
Washington, DC.

The subcommittee met, pursuant to notice, at 2:00 p.m., in room 2200 Rayburn House Office Building, Hon. Christopher H. Smith (chairman of the subcommittee) presiding.

Mr. SMITH. Subcommittee will come to order and good afternoon to everyone.

Over the past 20 years, much has changed in Vietnam. Some Vietnamese are a little richer, but universally recognized human rights remain elusive for most.

The Vietnamese Communist Party has opened up a bit to the outside world but remains closed to the idea of democracy and the rule of law. U.S.-Vietnamese relations have warmed because of Vietnam's fears of China's increasing economic power and its incursions into the South China Sea.

But human rights improvements have not come from so-called better relations. The administration has included Vietnam, a dictatorship, among several democracies in the Trans-Pacific Partnership, granted potentially lucrative trade benefits to Communist leaders.

Shockingly, during his recent trip, President Obama gave up the U.S. arms embargo. In other words, the U.S. is poised to provide lethal weapons to a brutal dictatorship that jails and tortures dissidents.

Where are the background checks, Mr. President, of those soldiers and secret police who will have access to sophisticated weapons?

Who will monitor the use or abuse of these lethal weapons? What is triggered if U.S.-supplied weapons are used to commit atrocities?

The reality is that the administration chose to reward one of Asia's most repressive regimes with the region's most worst human rights record without getting any tangible progress on freedoms and liberties.

We did hear the administration touting the bilateral labor consistency plan. It's signed as part of the TPP. But as the submitted testimony by Jackie Bong Wright states, as of today independent labor unions remain prohibited. Labor activists are in jail and labor organizers are severely beaten.

That the Vietnamese also detained and prevented civil society activists from meeting President Obama during his visit was not just an insult to the President, it is a bare-fisted demonstration of Vietnam's repressive government.

His visit was an epic failure of diplomacy. The President has said repeatedly that he wants to rise above history and heal wounds with America's old adversaries.

But that is not done by signing bad deals with dictators, giving them lethal weapons, and getting nothing in return.

This is shortsighted, misguided, and driven by an ideological agenda more than a clear assessment of long-term U.S. interests. The end result of the President's visit is that the American people now get to subsidize the lifestyles of Communist Party leaders and underwrite their repression of religious communities and rights advocates.

Vietnamese-Americans have asked this Congress and the last three administrations to prioritize human rights concerns with Hanoi.

But a small group of Vietnam ''experts'' in Washington veto these plans, holding on to the mistaken belief that trade, investment, and engagement will bring about political reform.

Trade, investment, and engagement failed to change Vietnam in 2001, the bilateral trade agreement failed to bring reforms in 2007 when Vietnam joined the WTO, and it will fail now.

Just look at China for what will happen when authoritarian governments get rich. They get the resources they need to expand censorship and repression, to grow their secret police and military capabilities and, above all, to stay in power.

The President said famously in his inaugural address that if authoritarian countries would unclench their fists the U.S. would extend an open hand.

But I see no tangible evidence that Vietnam, Cuba, or Iran, for that matter, have unclenched their fists. In fact, just the opposite is true.

The President seems more interested in photo opportunities with dictators than standing up for persecuted individuals who share our desire for freedom, democracy, and human rights.

This is not smart diplomacy. It is a surrender of U.S. interests and values. Sadly, the President's legacy will be the propping up of a Communist old guard when he should be standing with the new generation of freedom advocates in Vietnam.

We should stand with the oppressed, not with the oppressor. We must stand in solidarity with them. Over 100 prisoners of conscience remain detained in Vietnam, including human rights lawyer Nguyen Van Dai.

I met with Nguyen Van Dai in Hanoi in 2005 and his courageous wife, Vu Minh Khanh, testified at a subcommittee hearing several weeks ago in anticipation of the President's trip.

Why did the administration not demand the release of Vu's husband and all of these other prisoners and do so in public? To be strong and bold yet diplomatic?

Father Ly was released into house arrest a few months prior to his sentence ending, and this is not a human rights breakthrough. Father Ly went into prison healthy and vigorous but emerged sickly and broken.

I met him years ago when he was under house arrest another time after being released from a long incarceration. He is an amazing Catholic priest like so many of the leaders of the religious communities including the Venerable Thich Quang Do with whom I also met with and he continues to be under pagoda arrest.

I have met with a broad spectrum of Vietnam's rights advocates, religious leaders, and activists and I know there is a younger generation of Vietnam—66 percent of Vietnam is under the age of 40—that looks to U.S. leadership.

They want the United States to push for political reforms and universally-recognized human rights. They hunger for the type of liberty and a life they see enjoyed by their relatives in New Jersey, California, Virginia, Texas, Louisiana, and in many other parts of this country and around the world—places where the Vietnamese diaspora have migrated and have flourished and have been great citizens.

It is for this reason that I am asking and making another push to pass legislation that I have authored known as the Vietnam Human Rights Act. This bill has passed four times only to be blocked in the Senate—first time back in the year 2004.

The bipartisan Vietnam Human Rights Act will restore the right priorities to U.S. policy toward Vietnam and will limit U.S. non-humanitarian assistance that goes to Vietnam until there are concrete human rights protections.

The bill also says that Vietnam should be designated as a Country of Particular Concern (CPC) for its religious freedom violations. Just last week, I chaired a hearing, and Dan will remember it well.

We had the Ambassador-at-Large for International Religious Freedom and the former Chairman of the U.S. Commission on International Religious Freedom and the Commission has made a very strong and consistent appeal to the IRF office to put Vietnam in that CPC category.

It had been taken off prematurely during an economic agreement in the false hope that there would be deliverables that never happened.

People who came forward including those who signed Bloc 8406, a wonderful human rights manifesto, found themselves targeted because they signed on and did so openly in the belief that somehow after the agreement with the United States there would be a new era. That era has not happened.

We all know that CPC designation worked when it was used by the Bush administration but, again, I believe that the Bush administration lifted it prematurely in anticipation of, but without, concrete changes made.

The Communist Party is not Vietnam's future. That future lies with the Nguyen Van Dais and many other advocates of political reform and human rights who seek our freedoms more than our trade.

U.S. policy must send the unmistakable message to the Government of Vietnam that human rights improvements are important to better relations critically linked to our mutual economic and security interests and will not be ignored nor will they be bargained away.

The President failed to send this message. It is up to the Congress and the next administration, although there are some months remaining in this one, to restore the right priorities to the U.S.-Vietnam relations.

I would like to now yield to my friend, Mr. Donovan, for any comments.

Mr. DONOVAN. Thank you, Mr. Chairman.

I would like to yield my time to give the witnesses more time to testify. I look forward to their testimony and to their insight into the relations between our country and theirs.

Mr. SMITH. Thank you.

I would like to now welcome our distinguished witnesses to the witness table, beginning first with Pastor Rmah Loan, who is a Montagnard pastor with Christian Missionary Alliance and later became chaplain of a Montagnard church that is affiliated with the Southern Evangelical Church of Vietnam. His church has 36,000 followers and the authorities often showcase it to foreign missions that visit central highlands. Pastor Loan was the head of his church only in title.

The government put in place an administrative committee to oversee all operations of the church. It made all decisions and Pastor Loan had no say whatsoever. Every statement of Pastor Loan must be vetted by this committee and preapproved by the proper security apparatus.

In June 2014, Pastor Loan and his wife came to the United States at the invitation of a local church but they have not returned under the threat of arrest.

We will then hear from Ms. Katie Duong, who is the overseas representative of the Popular Bloc of Cao Dai Religion, also a member of the Advisory Committee for Religious Freedom in Vietnam.

Until recently, her father, Mr. Duong Xuan Luong, a senior member of the Popular Bloc of Cao Dai, continued to lead it in Vietnam, facing increasing threats by local authorities who fled to Thailand early this year but has continued to lead and advocate for the Popular Bloc of Cao Dai Religion and has filed multiple reports on violations of freedom of religion to the U.N. Special Rapporteur on freedom of religion or belief.

We will then hear from Dr. Nguyen Dinh Thang, who I have known for 25 years or more. Dr. Thang came to the United States as a refugee from Vietnam in 1979.

After earning his Ph.D. he began volunteering at Boat People SOS in 1988. Now serving as head of Boat People SOS, Dr. Thang has worked for the past 25 years to resettle 20,000 boat people to the U.S. after they were rescued from Vietnam and also has worked to rescue more than 4,000 victims of trafficking.

He has received numerous awards for his extensive work on human rights. He travels extensively to Asia and I would note parenthetically on the boat people it was Dr. Thang who alerted this subcommittee.

It resulted in four hearings including a closed briefing with the administration in the hopes that they would reform their efforts to send so many back who had been found to be real refugees. And as a direct result of his leadership, those 20,000 people came in under the ROVR program and had it not been for him that would not have happened.

So thank you. Those families are deeply appreciative as am I and this subcommittee for your leadership.

Then we welcome back again Mr. T. Kumar, who is Amnesty International's director for international advocacy. He has testified many times before the U.S. Congress on human rights abuses.

He has served as a human rights monitor in many Asian countries as well as Bosnia, Afghanistan, Guatemala, Sudan, and South Africa. He has also served as director of several refugee ships and camps. T. Kumar was a political prisoner himself for 5 years in Sri Lanka for his peaceful human rights activities.

Amnesty International adopted him as a prisoner of conscience and now he, on the leadership side, tried to help many others and to rescue many others from that cruel fate.

I would like to yield to Chairman Rohrabacher if he has any opening comments.

Mr. ROHRABACHER. I am upset at this administration but I have to be fair to this administration when I say that. I have been upset with other administrations as well, Republican and Democratic, when it comes to issues like being serious about human rights.

American leaders can sit right next to tyrants and gangsters and not even bring up the fact that they have a one-child policy, for example, in China where millions of babies were being murdered.

And in the case of Vietnam, you know, and we have a President who can go to Vietnam but can't go see General Sisi in Egypt. That tells us something.

The Government of Vietnam is in no way consistent with what the American people believe is honest government and consistent with any of the principles of democracy that we believe in.

And this administration has just basically closed their eyes to those particular fundamentals that are supposed to be the basis of our own Government. Well, if we don't believe in it enough to bring this up and make that a major issue of contention between our governments, what does that say about our own beliefs in our own system here?

So, Mr. Chairman, again, I always admire your willingness to spend your time and your effort to focus on the fundamental issue that really counts and that is whether we respect the human rights of the people of whatever country it is and whether we expect those governments to maintain a certain standard.

Vietnam is nowhere near that standard and the United States needs to say so aggressively and if indeed they want to make things better we should work with them and try to make it better.

But at this point, they certainly haven't come close, and thank you for holding this hearing today.

Mr. SMITH. Thank you, Chairman Rohrabacher.

Pastor Loan.

STATEMENT OF PASTOR RMAH LOAN (FORMER HEAD, SOUTHERN EVANGELICAL CHURCH OF VIETNAM—DAK NONG PROVINCE)

[The following statement was delivered through an interpreter.]

Pastor LOAN. The Honorable Christopher Smith, distinguished Members of Congress, my name is Rmah Loan. I was born on February 12th, 1950. I have been a pastor for 44 years under the Southern Evangelist Church of Vietnam.

From 1967 to 1969, I assisted American special forces during the Vietnam War. Afterward, I went to biblical school in Ban Me Thuot to study theology.

I worked as a pastor in residence for 2 years until I was detained by the Communist force in 1975. I was imprisoned for 8 years.

I was in jail for 8 years because of my Christian belief and support for the United States Armed Forces. After my release from prison, I remained under house arrest until 1986.

In 1986, I was appointed by the Southern Evangelical Christians of Southern Vietnam to be in charge of the Evangelical Church in Budak village where I remained until 2014.

In 2014, I came to the United States for church-related business but then found out I could return to Vietnam in safety. Now I am asking this great nation to grant me asylum because if I return to Vietnam I will be imprisoned again, tortured, and even killed.

Today, I would like to tell you about my church in Budak, Thuan An, Dak Mil, Dak Nong Province. This church serves approximately 100,000 followers throughout Dak Nong Province that includes ethnic Bunong, Hmong, Giao, San Chi, Nung, Tay, and Kinh.

In 2007, Hanoi allowed the congregation to build the church in Budak. Even though we have a church, we do not have the freedom to practice our religion. The Vietnamese Government controls the executive committee that leads the church.

Any time we want to hold elections for the executive committee, we have to inform the subdistrict, district, and the Dak Nong Province police to request their permission.

The church must provide full names of our candidates for background checks. To be eligible, a candidate must not have been in service of the South Vietnam Government or a member of the FULRO, United Front for the Liberation of Oppressed Races, or any deemed to be opposed to the Hanoi Government.

On election day, the government authorities preside over the election process. The government authorities also attend and observe all ordination ceremonies.

When the church wants to celebrate holidays such as Christmas, Easter or for a wedding or a funeral service, the pastor must get prior permission from the authorities—the specific date, time, duration of the service, as well as the number of participants.

The pastor must provide the text of his sermon to the government 7 days before the service for prior approval. The government even controls the words that we can use in our sermon.

It is forbidden to use such words as devil because in Vietnamese ''ma quy'' can be flipped around to spell ''My qua'' meaning that Americans are coming back. For such absurd reasons, we may not mention devil in our sermon.

Similarly, we may not say that Christ is coming again because the authorities interpret that as meaning Americans will return to Vietnam.

The Vietnamese Government accused Protestantism to be an American religion, neither may we use the word freedom because the government believes that freedom refers to America, as in the Land of the Free.

The authorities also send their operatives to come and monitor our services. At the start of the service, the program leader must recognize and give thanks to the Communist Party and government officials first and then we can give thanks to the Lord, the guests and the church, in that order.

In 2014, my wife and I came to the United States at the invitation of a local church. As soon as we were in the country, we received notice from a fellow pastor in Vietnam advising me not to return because the authorities were investigating my children about our whereabouts.

The authorities suspect that I had disclosed to the world the death by torture of a Hmong member of my church. In 2013, Hoang Van Ngai, a faithful and dedicated deacon at our church, was detained and beaten to death.

The authorities ordered me to never mention this incident and threatened my life if I dare to defy their order. In 2014, news about Deacon Ngai's death by torture became known to the world.

The authorities suspect that I was the source of information. I was not. Regardless, if I return to Vietnam now, I will be detained, tortured and likely killed the same way they killed Deacon Hoang Van Ngai.

It has not been easy on me and my wife because our children are left in Vietnam. I am applying for asylum in the United States but it can take years for my fate to be decided.

America is the land that was founded in religious freedom. Just like the immigrants and refugees from hundreds of years ago, I have reached the shore of America, seeking safety and freedom.

I ask that you, as the leaders of the United States, to never forget that millions of people around the world are suffering every day all because of the god they believe in. I ask that you continue to protect them and also that you protect my wife and me so we do not have to face persecution in the hands of Vietnamese authorities.

We believe President Obama and leaders of the free world must have a road map for peace, freedom and democracy for Vietnam.

We must stand with one voice, one heart, and one task, working together to defend the rights of religious freedom for Montagnard Evangelical Christians and all Vietnamese citizens in Vietnam.

Thank you for the privilege to speak freely for the first time in 41 years. Thank you for remembering the Montagnard people and taking a stand for our survival. May God bless you and the United States of America.

May God bless you and the United States of America.

Thank you for the time to speak and my chance to be here in America. I want to stay here so I can save my life.

[The prepared statement of Pastor Loan follows:]

Restrictions on and Repression of Religious Freedom in Vietnam

Statement of Pastor Rmah Loan

before

The House Foreign Relations Committee
Subcommittee on Subcommittee on Africa, Global Health, Global Human Rights, and International Organizations

Hearing entitled "The President's Visit to Vietnam: A Missed Opportunity to Advance Human Rights" on June 22, 2016

The Honorable Christopher Smith
Distinguished members of Congress

My name is Loan Rmah. I was born on February 12, 1950 and has been a pastor for 44 years under the Southern Evangelist Church of Vietnam.

From 1967-1969, I assisted American Special Forces during the Vietnam War.

After the war I went to Biblical School in Ban Me Thuot to study theology.

I worked as a Pastor in residence for two years until I was detained by the Communist forces in 1975. I was imprisoned for eight years because of my Christian faith and my support to the United States armed forces.

After my release from prison I remained under house arrest until 1986.

In 1986 I was appointed by the SECV to be in charge of the Evangelical Church at Budak Village, where I remained until 2014. In 2014 I came to the United States for church-related business but then found out that I could return to Vietnam in safety. Now I am asking that this great nation to grant me asylum because if I return to Vietnam, I will be imprisoned again, tortured, and even killed.

Today I would like to tell you about my Church in Budak, Thuan An, DakMil, Daknong Province. This Church serves approximately 100,000 followers throughout Daknong Province. They include ethnic Bunong, Hmong, Giao, San chi, Nung, Tay and Kinh.

In 2007 Hanoi allowed our Congregation to build the church in Budak.

Even though we have a church, we do not have the freedom to practice our religion. The The Vietnamese government controls the Executive Committee that leads the church. Anytime we want to hold elections of the Executive Committee, we have to inform the Sub-district, District and Daknong Province Police to request their permission. The Church must provide them the full names of all candidates for background check. To be eligible, a candidate must not have been in service of the South Vietnamese Government, or a member of the FULRO (United Front for the Liberation of Oppressed Races) movement or any group deemed to be opposing the Hanoi Government. On election date, the government authority presides over the election process. The government authority also attends and observes all ordination ceremonies.

When the church wants to celebrate holidays such as Christmas or Easter, or offer wedding or funeral services, the Pastor must get prior permission from the authority and specify the day, time and duration of the services as well as the number of participants. The Pastor must provide the text of his sermon to the government seven days before the services for prior approval.

The government even controls the words that we can use in our sermons. It is forbidden to use words such as "devil" because in Vietnamese "ma quy" can be flipped around to spell as "My qua", meaning that Americans coming back. For such an absurd reason, we may not mention "devil" in our sermons. Similarly, we may not say "The Christ is coming again" because the authority interprets that as meaning "Americans will return to Vietnam." The Vietnamese government accuses Protestantism to be an American religion. Neither may we use the word "freedom" because the government believes that freedom refers to America as in the "land of the free".

The authorities also send their operatives to come and monitor our religious services. At the start of the services, the program leader must recognize and give thanks to the Communist Party and government officials first. Then we can give thanks the Lord, the guests and the Church, in that order.

In 2014, my wife and I came to the United States at the invitation of a local church. Soon I received notices from fellow pastors in Vietnam advising me not to return because the authorities were investigating my children about our whereabouts. The authorities suspected that I had disclosed to the world the death by torture of a Hmong member of my Church.

In 2013, Hoang Van Ngai, a faithful and dedicate deacon at our church, was detained and beaten to death. The authorities ordered me to never mention this incident and threatened my life if I dare to defy their order. In 2014, news about Deacon Ngai's death by torture became known to the world. The authorities suspected that I was the source of information. I was not.

Regardless, I return to Vietnam now, I will be detained, tortured, and likely killed the same way they killed Deacon Hoang Van Ngai.

It has not been easy on me and my wife because our children are left in Vietnam. I am applying for asylum in the United States but it could take years for my fate to be decided.

America is a land that was founded on religious freedom. Just like the immigrants and refugees from hundreds of years ago, I have reached the shores of America seeking safety and freedom.

I ask that you, as leaders of the United States, to never forget that millions of people around the world are suffering every day, all because of the God they believe in. I ask that you continue to protect them and also that you protect my wife and me so we do not face persecution in the hands of the Vietnamese authorities.

We believe President Obama and leaders of the free world must have a road map for peace, freedom and democracy for Vietnam. We must not allow the yoke of persecution imposed on Christians and followers of other faith to continue. We must stand with one voice, one heart and one task: Working together to defend the right to religious freedom for Montagnard Evangelical Christians and all Vietnamese citizens in Vietnam.

Thank you for the privilege to speak freely for the first time in the past 41 years. Thank you for remembering the Montagnard people and taking a stand for our survival.

May God bless you and the United States of America.

———————

Mr. SMITH. Pastor Loan, thank you for your very courageous and compelling testimony. It really is extremely helpful that the American public, this subcommittee, the Congress, hear what you just said as well as our other witnesses. So on behalf of all of us, thank you so very much.

I would like to now recognize Ms. Duong. Please present your testimony.

STATEMENT OF MS. KATIE DUONG, OVERSEAS REPRESENTATIVE, POPULAR BLOC OF CAO DAI RELIGION

Ms. DUONG. Good afternoon, ladies and gentlemen, Mr. Chairman and distinguished Members of Congress. My name is Katie Duong Skiba and it is my honor to be here today to present about my religion, Cao Dai, which is a very small religion founded in Vietnam in 1926.

Now, we Cao Dai people call for unity, love, peace and respect for all other faiths and we have our own faith, rituals, and traditions. However, the Communists—the Vietnamese Communist Government has been trying to change everything.

And my presentation today will have three parts—government takeover, ongoing persecutions, and request for support.

So the government took over our main temple after 1975 and disbanded all the leadership's organization and they basically told us to go home. And after that they confiscated our main temple and all other temples, and after a while they appointed their people—the Communist people—to control the temple and the whole Cao Dai Religion.

They changed our rituals and they forced all of us to obey their disciplines, which we do not agree, and because of that we have been facing a lot of ongoing persecutions. And then I would like to show you a few pictures of the recent.

So since 1975, we have been facing, you know, government takeover and we have been trying so hard to get together and tell the government that we need religious freedom—give us the right—give us back the temple.

This happened in May last year when almost 1,000 people went back to the temple asking them to let us hold a meeting to elect our own leaders instead of them forcing the Communist leader on us.

And they basically banned us from approaching the temple, and I can show you a lot of people who could not get into the premises. And it's kind of dark but you can see the man was arrested and these women have paint on their ao dai, which is the traditional dress that the Cao Dai people wear.

So these are things that happened and at a funeral if we don't let the Communist Cao Dai come to host the ceremony they will attack us. And you see that this is the funeral—the ceremony that we had and, you know, got destroyed, basically.

And this is the Divine Eye installation which is a very important ceremony that people have—religion have to install that at their house. You see the first picture there's a picture of the Divine Eye.

But the second picture of the Divine Eye portrait was taken away by those people. That is a very insulting action and they basically came in and we closed the door and they tried to get in. They attacked us and this has been, like, ongoing.

It is not one incident. It has been going on and on and on. We got hurt. People got imprisoned and vandalism and people got arrested in the van or truck.

Do you see that? In the last picture on the bottom right corner, people was arrested to the government offices just because we are practicing our religion.

And these documents show that these people could not get out of the country because they are trying to go to Thailand to attend their Asian Religious Freedom Forum.

So we have all different kinds of persecutions and ongoing violations for religious freedom. A personal example would be my family and my father.

He was arrested and put into jail when I was 15 and my younger sister was only 10. My mother had to take care of the whole family of four children by herself and with a lot of difficulty financially caused by the government.

And then after getting out of prison, my father continued to fight for religious freedoms and then—and they continued to harass him. In 2008, they tried to arrest him again to put him in jail.

But, luckily, he was not at home and they have been trying to arrest him since then, and recently they have been given threats again. So my father has to, you know, get out of the country. As a U.S. citizen I have sponsored my father and my mother to come with me to the United States.

My mom could come with me but my father, unfortunately, the Vietnamese Government refused to give him a passport or any documentation to go through the visa process.

My last section will be our request for support. If possible, we would love to remain independent from the government control.

We don't want any interference from the government and we want to reserve our culture the unique way that we practice our religions. In order to do so we have to have freedom of, you know, movement, freedom of assembly, association, freedom of speech, and information.

We want the Vietnamese Government to respect human rights, especially religious freedom rights that they have signed for the universal agreement with the United Nations.

And with the growing bilateral development connection between the U.S. Government and the Vietnamese Government, the U.S. Government has solid ground to remind the Vietnamese Government to respect that and that is a value that the U.S. has been living on. So we look forward to that and I appreciate your time.

I appreciate your concern and we, the Cao Dai people, really need and appreciate it.

Thank you.

[The prepared statement of Ms. Duong follows:]

Statement of Katie Duong
Overseas Representative
Popular Council of Cao Dai Religion

Before
US House of Representatives. Committee on Foreign Affairs. Subcommittee on Africa, Global Health, Global Human Rights, and International Organizations.
Hearing entitled *"The President's Visit to Vietnam: A Missed Opportunity to Advance Human Rights"* on June 22, 2016.

CAODAISM: ESTABLISHMENT AND GOVERNMENT TAKEOVER

Third Amnesty of God or Đại Đạo Tam Kì Phổ Độ, also known as Caodaism or Cao Dai Religion, is an endogenous religion founded in South Vietnam in 1926. Caodaism calls for unity, love, justice, peace, freedom, democracy and respects for all faiths. Our faith also requires that we follow and obey our religion's code or rules, but the Vietnamese Communist Party has forced Caodaist disciples to follow its policies and to abandon our Religious Constitution established by God, including our laws, traditional rituals and our organizing bodies and institutions.

Prior to the fall of the Republic of Vietnam in April 1975, all religious activities of Caodaism were managed by three Councils: Popular Council, Sacerdotal Council and Superior Council. They had the power to make or modify religious laws/rules, and the combined power of the three Councils was equal to God's power. All laws/rules must be ratified by the three Councils, who then submit them to the Supreme Being for final approval -- all positions of Caodaist dignitaries must be approved by God and Divine Spirits through spiritist séances.

In 1979, the Communist regime disbanded the Sacerdotal Council of the Caodai Tayninh Holy See; dissolved all Cao Dai Religious Administrations from the central to local levels; and established the Governance Council (Hoi Dong Chuong Quan), an entity under the government's control. Forty of the forty-six religious properties belonging to the Tayninh Holy See were confiscated. Some of the properties were demolished, some were misused, and some were left vacant. The government appointed the Cao Dai Governance Council and Communist Party members to run all confiscated properties. In 1997, the government-created Governance Council modified Caodai's canonical laws and traditional rituals to allow them to take control of all religious activities of Cao Dai religion. We independent Cao Daiists call them the "Cao Dai 1997 Sect". Cao Dai followers who do not submit themselves to this sect are banned from practicing their religion.

I am a member of the Popular Council of Cao Dai Religion. We re-established the Popular Council of Cao Dai Religion in 2008 in order to eventually restore the true Cao Dai religion that was founded in 1926. We do not accept the leadership of Cao Dai 1997 Sect. We have been asking the government to let us elect our own leaders and restore our religion. Repression and persecution is the answer that we received.

DIFFICULTIES FACED TODAY: KEY INCIDENTS SINCE 2015

Below are some examples illustrating the ongoing persecution against independent Cao Dai followers.

CaoDai Tayninh Holy See, Tay Ninh – May 2015

More than 900 members of Cao Dai Popular Council signed a petition to the government to hold a general assembly meeting at the Cao Dai Holy See in Tay Ninh on May 27, 2015 for independent Cao Dai members to elect their own religious leaders. When these members gathered for the meeting, police officers and authorities barricaded the gates, blocking them from entering the temple's premises. The police attacked some members, arrested some others, and dispersed the rest. The meeting did not materialize because of so many interruptions and obstacles put in place by the government.

Cu Chi, Ho Chi Minh City – June 2015

Cao Dai Popular Council members gathered to discuss the articles published in a Vietnamese state-run magazine related to the failed May 2015 meeting; the article described the meeting as an illegal act of rebels. The meeting was held at the house of Mr. and Mrs. Vo in Củ Chi County, HCMC. The People's Committee of Cu Chi County sent its agents to disband the meeting. Later that day, it delivered a "Notice on prohibition of illegal propaganda" to the residence of Mr. and Mrs. Vo.

Trang Bang, Tay Ninh – July 2015

Cao Dai members gathered at the home of Mrs. Nguyen Thi Kim Thoi in Trang Bang District, Tay Ninh Province to attend the private ceremony to install the Divine Eye portrait at her home's altar. A Commune police officer in uniform came to the site to direct a mob assault against the attendants. They smashed the furniture and demolished the Divine Eye portrait.

Hoa Thanh, Tay Ninh – November 2015

Cao Dai members gathered at the house of Mrs. Phạm Kim Anh in Hòa Thành District, Tây Ninh Province for the ceremony marking the final period of mourning for an adherent. Members of the Cao Dai 1997 Sect came to the site with the commune police. They used megaphones to order Cao Dai worshippers to leave the ceremony area. They then proceeded to overturn tables full of food, vandalize ceremony decorations and furniture, and damage part of the house. They also forced the homeowner to follow them to People's Committee office, where he was detained for several hours. The victim was let go only after many Cao Daiists showed up to demand his release.

Go Dau, Tay Ninh – November 2015

Cao Dai members gathered at the household of Mrs. Cao Thi Chinh, in Go Dau District, Tay Ninh Province to attend the rite of installing the Divine Eye portrait at her home's altar. The Cao Dai 1997 Sect sent its members and thugs to interrupt the ceremony. They destroyed furniture and decorations, trashed the food, confiscated phones and cameras of attendants, and ordered them to end the rituals.

Binh Duong, Tay Ninh – March 2016

Cao Dai member Duong Xuan Luong (who has been under warrant arrest since 2008) received a threat from the police that he would be arrested anytime unless he cooperated with the government and stopped advocacy for religious freedom. The threat was real and imminent because he had been imprisoned before for 30 months. He had to flee to Thailand for safety and is seeking refugee status with the United Nations. He is my father. As U.S. citizen, I sponsored him and my mother to come to the United States. However, only my mother could leave Vietnam to join me. The Vietnamese government refused to issue my father a passport or any travel document in order to go through the immigrant visa process.

Vinh Long, Tien Giang, Long An – Vietnam – May 2016

Seven members from Cao Dai Popular Council in 3 provinces were threatened by the government authorities and ordered to stop all contact and cooperation with Dr. Nguyen Dinh Thang, President and CEO of BPSOS, or they will be arrested. The government officers falsely accused that Dr. Nguyen Dinh Thang aims to overthrow the Vietnamese government, and therefore whoever connected with him will be arrested. These Cao Dai members attended the Conference on Freedom of Religion or Belief in Southeast Asia in Bangkok, Thailand last September and/or participated in training sessions on how to report violations of religious freedom to the United Nations. Both activities were organized by BPSOS.

ONGOING PERSECUTION

Cao Dai members who do not submit themselves to the government-controlled Cao Dai 1997 Sect face the following forms of persecution:

- Loss of freedom of movement: Prominent Cao Dai members such as Tran Quoc Tien, Vo Van Quang, Tran Ngoc Suong, Nguyen Xuan Mai, Nguyen Van Thiet, and Luong Thi No have been placed under travel ban.
- Impending arrest: At least one Cai Dai follower, my own father, has not been able to stay in any one place for long due to personal safety since an arrest warrant was issued against him in 2008. He had to get out of Vietnam and currently seeks refugee status in Thailand.
- Threats to livelihood: Local authorities have used different ploys and obstacles to negatively affect the businesses, employment and income-earning activities of Cao Dai practitioners deemed to be non-compliant to the Cao Dai 1997 Sect.
- Harassment: Many Cao Dai followers receive multiple "invitations to work" with the commune police officers, which practically constitutes arbitrary short-term detention, and are monitored by the police on a daily basis regarding what they do, where they go, and who they meet.

PLAN OF ACTIONS AND REQUEST FOR SUPPORT

As Cao Dai followers, we wish to retain our independence from government control and be able to practice our religion as we see fit. To do so, we aim to hold a Popular Meeting to elect our leaders and to reform our own religious organization. In order to achieve this ultimate goal, we need freedoms of movement, assembly and association. We also need freedoms of speech and information, and the right to retain and practice our unique culture and traditions. These are rights stated in the **Universal Declaration of Human Rights** and further enshrined in the many legally binding treaty bodies to which Vietnam is a party. Freedom of religion includes these other rights and the Vietnamese government must not only allow us to exercise these rights but promote and protect them.

In pursuit of our goal, we are seeking support from independent religious communities and civil society organizations in Vietnam to pressure the government to uphold its binding human rights obligations and not interfere with our Popular Meeting to elect our own leaders.

We are also seeking international support, especially from the U.S. government. With expanding bilateral relations with Vietnam, the U.S. government has solid ground to demand that the Vietnamese government live up to its obligations to respecting and protecting human rights, including our right to religious freedom.

We ask civil society around the world to endorse and support our efforts to re-establish the organizational structure of our religion as established in 1926, and to raise their voice of concern to the Vietnamese government on our behalf so that we can enjoy freedom of religion in the near future.

Thank you for your time and support. We, independent Cao Dai followers, urgently need and highly appreciate it.

Sincerely,

On behalf of

The Popular Council of Cao Dai Religion in Vietnam – Washington DC June 22, 2016.

Mr. SMITH. Ms. Duong, thank you very much for your testimony, for detailing in your written submission seven specific instances which give greater detail as to the pervasiveness of these actions—and these were instances in 2015—which, of course, continue to today.

And without objection, your full statement and that of all of our distinguished witnesses will be made a part of the record. But thank you for your witness.

Ms. DUONG. Thank you, Mr. Chairman.

Mr. SMITH. Dr. Thang.

STATEMENT OF NGUYEN DINH THANG, PH.D., PRESIDENT AND CHIEF EXECUTIVE OFFICER, BOAT PEOPLE SOS

Mr. THANG. Mr. Chairman and distinguished members of the committee, thank you for holding this hearing at this very critical time about missed opportunities to advance freedoms for 93 million Vietnamese people.

As the previous speakers have said very well, the situation of religions in Vietnam remains very dire and deplorable. President Obama could have used his recent state visit to Vietnam to at least try to curb the backsliding in human rights in that country.

He could have insisted that Vietnam release a significant number of prisoners of conscience before announcing the lifting of the arms embargo. That didn't happen.

He could have challenged the leadership of Vietnam to answer the people's demand for transparency in the case of 80 tons of dead fish as a gesture showing commitment to the environmental protection which, by the way, is a requirement under the Trans-Pacific Partnership, or TPP, and he didn't speak out on that issue either.

President Obama could have demanded unhindered access to individuals he wanted to meet comparable to the level of access accorded to the Vietnamese President when he visited here in the States. Or President Obama could have called on authorities to honor the Convention Against Torture, which the National Assembly of Vietnam just ratified by, investigating and prosecuting known violators, and there are many of them.

President Obama didn't do any of the above, disappointingly. Of the hundreds of prisoners of conscience, only Father Nguyen Van Ly was released and only by 10 weeks in advance of the end of his term of imprisonment.

Hundreds of peaceful pro-environment protestors were arrested, detained and some were even beaten the weekend before and after the President's state visit to Vietnam. Civil society members invited to meet with the President were confined to their homes or even kidnapped.

On top of that, two American citizens were abducted and detained, and by the way, one of them is here in this room—Miss Dolly Khuu. She was one of the American citizens kidnapped and detained in Vietnam.

The President brought home to America a $11.3 billion deal for Boeing, which is great. However, nothing for human rights, and the backsliding has accelerated of late.

In just 1 week, 3 months ago—in just 1 week, four bloggers and three land rights activists were sentenced to a total of 33 years of imprisonment.

Many former prisoners of conscience who were only recently released from prison or house detention have been rearrested such as—and you know him very well, Mr. Chairman—lawyer Nguyen Van Dai, land rights activist Can Thi Theu and pro-democracy advocate Tran Anh Kim.

Many independent religious communities are facing increasingly brutal repression. Last August, a Hmong Christian was arrested the day after his meeting with members of the U.S. Commission on International Freedom (USCIRF).

He was brutally tortured for 2 days and had to be hospitalized because he had met with the U.S. delegation and in January of this year a Montagnard pastor died from injuries caused by torture by the police.

A fellow Montagnard pastor reported this death at a meeting with Ambassador David Saperstein last month. He himself was arrested and interrogated for 2 days.

His interrogators threatened him with disappearance and harm to his wife and children if he did not stop reporting violations and did not renounce his faith.

Mrs. Tran Thi Hong, the wife of imprisoned Lutheran Pastor Nguyen Cong Chinh and a human rights defender herself, was also arrested after her meeting with Ambassador Saperstein.

She was subjected to repeated beatings and torture. Her daily ''working'' session with the police was suspended just before the arrival of President Obama to Vietnam but resumed immediately after his departure.

I am glad to say that now it has stopped, thanks to the very strong intervention from Ambassador Saperstein himself. And let me show the picture of Mrs. Hong here.

This is Pastor Nguyen Cong Chinh. He himself was brutalized several years ago before his imprisonment and this is Mrs. Hong, after the torture session—she was dumped in front of her house.

She couldn't walk at all. She couldn't stand up. The neighbors passing by found her on the street and dragged her home. And this is her, Mrs. Hong, and the injuries to her knees and legs and feet and hands.

And this is another incident of torture and you can see bruises and red marks on her face, and this is how the Vietnamese Government treated people who have met with U.S. delegations.

And I believe it is an affront to our Government that President Obama didn't raise that issue, didn't condemn the Government of Vietnam to have done such things.

And in the light of all these disturbing trends, somehow our administration still hangs its hope on Vietnam's promise to pass its first law on religion.

Its latest draft would only cement the status quo and even make it worse by creating more bureaucratic layers of registration requirements and by completely eliminating the one section that was good in previous drafts.

That was the section on compliance with international standards. That section had been removed in the latest draft of that law.

Unless fundamentally and drastically modified, having no law at all would be a lesser evil.

In early 2007, the Vietnamese Government launched a brutal political clamp down against dissidents and religious leaders right after it had gotten all it wanted, namely accession to the WTO, the lifting of the CPC designation, permanent normal trade relation status with the U.S. and playing host to the APEC Summit.

The situation now is strikingly and disturbingly similar to then. Vietnam just got the U.S. arms embargo lifted, the TPP signed, and it will host again the APEC Summit next year.

It is therefore critical that Congress now acts so as to avert the repeat of the 2007 fiasco by demanding that Vietnam be redesignated a Country of Particular Concern and that violators of religious freedom be placed under a U.S. visa ban, by enacting legislation which—with stricter monitoring and reporting requirements and more effective sanctions against human rights abusers, by delaying the ratification of TPP to allow for sufficient time to test Vietnam's willingness and resolve to honor labor rights, environmental protection and freedom of religion, to end torture and to combat modern-day slavery, by making any future sale of lethal weapons contingent on Vietnam's release of all prisoners of conscience, by giving Vietnam's civil society—and this is very important—recognition and legitimacy through direct dialogue with its representatives of civil society networks such as Bloc 8406, Vietnamese Independent Civil Society Organizations Network, or VICSON, and Vietnam Multi-faith Roundtable, which was just recently formed, and finally, by coordinating intervention efforts with parliamentarians of other countries.

There are many of them in Europe as well as in ASEAN who would be very much interested in working and collaborating with U.S. Members of Congress.

With that, I thank you again, Mr. Chairman and Members of Congress.

[The prepared statement of Mr. Thang follows:]

Nguyen Dinh Thang, PhD

President & CEO, BPSOS

Spokesperson, Coalition for a Free and Democratic Vietnam

Testimony at Congressional Hearing on

"The President's Visit to Vietnam: A Missed Opportunity to Advance Human Rights"

Subcommittee on Africa, Global Health, Global Human Rights, and International Organizations

Committee on Foreign Affairs

House of Representatives

June 22, 2016

Mr. Chairman and distinguished members of the Committee:

Thank you for holding this hearing at this time. Exactly a month has passed since President Obama announced, in Ha Noi, the total lifting of the U.S. arms embargo against Vietnam. Vietnam offered no human rights concession in return. It is therefore important for Congress to take action and ensure that further expansion of partnership with Vietnam will promote our core values of liberty and human dignity.

President Obama could have insisted that ending the arms embargo be contingent on the unconditional and immediate release of political and religious prisoners. That was not the case. And we saw the rise in the number of arrests and prison sentences in the months preceding his trip to Vietnam.

President Obama could have used the recent environmental disaster that had resulted in 80 million tons of dead fish to test the Vietnamese authorities' commitments to the environmental protection clause of the Trans-Pacific Partnership. That clause requires government's transparency and public participation. Responding to popular demand for transparency, the Vietnamese government arrested hundreds of peaceful protesters the weekends before and after the President's state visit. Many of them were bloodily assaulted by the police.

As a public affront to the United States, Vietnamese police blocked or kidnapped civil society activists who had been invited to a personal meeting with President Obama in Ha Noi. The following day in Saigon, they arrested a college student while he was waiting in line, with invitation letter in hand, for a town meeting with President Obama. President Obama could have insisted on "no interference" as condition of his state visit, but he did not.

President Obama could have spoken out against the persecution of independent religious communities, especially because such persecution had been intentionally conducted in plain sight and in the face of our government.

Last August, Mr. Ma Van Pa, a Hmong Christian, was arrested the day after his meeting with commissioners of the U.S. Commission on International Religious Freedom (USCIRF) in Tuyen Quang Province. For two days he was subjected to torture – the police wanted to know what had been shared with the U.S. delegation. He suffered severe head injuries and had to be hospitalized.

Then in March of this year, Montagnard Pastor Y Nuen Ayun was arrested after having met with U.S. Ambassador David Saperstein. Thanks to listening devices, the police knew that he had reported the death by torture of a fellow Montagnard pastor two months earlier. At the end of two days of interrogation, the police told him that they can make him disappear and harm his wife and children anytime.

Mrs. Tran Thi Hong, the wife of imprisoned Lutheran Pastor Nguyen Cong Chinh and a human rights defender herself, fared even worse. Two weeks after Ambassador Saperstein had visited her at her home in Kontum, the police subjected her to repeated beatings and torture. Her meeting with the U.S. Ambassador violated Vietnam's law, she was told. Her daily "working" session with the police was suspended just prior to President Obama's arrival and resumed immediately after his departure. It stopped in early June, after strong intervention by the U.S. State Department and our embassy in Vietnam.

I believe it's not pure coincidence that persecution has increased in recent months. The government wants to prove to the Vietnamese people, particularly human rights advocates, that it can get all the benefits it wants from the United States without making any concessions on human rights in return. Unfortunately, President Obama's Vietnam visit has lent credibility to that message.

Testifying before this same Committee last week, Ambassador Saperstein correctly pointed out that, in the context of Vietnam, promises are meaningless without verifiable implementation. Problematically, the Vietnamese government only makes vague and unverifiable promises.

As you may remember, Mr. Chairman, in 2006 Ambassador John Hanford recommended lifting the CPC designation for Vietnam because its government had agreed to a long list of promises. But Vietnam insisted that these promises be kept confidential, which made verification practically impossible.

A fiasco ensued. The Vietnamese government issued Ordinance on Belief and Religion and the implementation decree. Both were designed to manage and control religious activities rather than to respect and protect the right to freedom of religion or belief. Yet the Bush Administration still lifted the CPC designation. A few months later, in early 2007, Vietnam turned around and brutally persecuted independent churches and religious communities. Hundreds of political dissidents and faith leaders were sent to prison, and the crackdown continues to this day.

It appears that we are setting ourselves up for a repeat of that catastrophic experience. The Vietnamese government now promises to pass its first law on religion. The current draft, however, would only cement the status quo and in certain aspects would even make it worse.

According to legal experts who examined this draft law, it maintains the government's approach of regulating and controlling religious affairs, lacks the necessary safeguards to protect against the abuse of power, and contains ambiguous language and administrative burdens. Compared to prior draft versions, the latest iteration is worse as it creates more bureaucratic layers of registration requirements and removes the section on compliance with international standards. Unless it is fundamentally and drastically modified, this draft law should be abandoned.

Fool me once shame on you, fool me twice shame on me. Let us not fall into that trap again. Congress can act to ensure that U.S. interest in human rights is an integral part of bilateral relations with Vietnam and improvements are measurable and verifiable, by:

(1) Requesting the Administration to duly enforce existing statutes, including to designate Vietnam as a country of particular concern and to place under visa ban Vietnamese government officials who have egregiously violated religious freedom;

(2) Enacting legislations with stricter monitoring and reporting requirements and more effective sanction measures against perpetrators of human rights abuses – such as the

Frank R. Wolf International Religious Freedom Act, the Vietnam Human Rights Sanctions Act, and the Vietnam Human Rights Act;

(3) Delaying the ratification of the Trans-Pacific Partnership (TPP) to allow time for a thorough study of Vietnam's intention to comply with its commitments to the right of workers to form free and independent unions, the right of all religious communities to practice their faith without interference or suppression, and environmental protection; and for the Vietnamese government to demonstrate good faith by freeing all prisoners of conscience unconditionally;

(4) Reaching out to and dialoguing directly with members of Vietnam's civil society and thus giving them the recognition that they deserve but have been denied by the Vietnamese government. This can be readily done with today's information and communication technologies. Tomorrow, as part of this year's Vietnam Advocacy Day, we will conference in a dozen of Vietnamese civil society leaders so that they can speak directly to interested members of Congress;

(5) Supporting civil society networks such as Bloc 8406, Vietnamese Independent Civil Society Organizations Network (VICSON), and Vietnam Multi-faith Roundtable. These networks represent Vietnam's budding civil society and their efforts to form a collective voice. They need recognition, visibility and protection. The more interactions they have with the U.S. government, UN agencies and international organizations, the less likely they will be crushed by the government;

(6) Coordinating intervention with established networks such as International Panel of Parliamentarians for Freedom of Religion or Belief or ASEAN Parliamentarians for Human Rights, or directly with individual like-minded members of parliaments. A number of German legislators have adopted prisoners of conscience in the model of the Tom Lantos Human Rights Commission's Defending Freedom Project, and some of them are actively working to free Lawyer Nguyen Van Dai; they would be interested in collaborating with U.S. members of Congress.

———————

Mr. SMITH. Dr. Thang, thank you so very much for your leadership and for your incisive comments today, which are very, very helpful. Thank you.

Mr. Kumar.

STATEMENT OF MR. T. KUMAR, DIRECTOR OF INTERNATIONAL ADVOCACY, AMNESTY INTERNATIONAL

Mr. KUMAR. Thank you very much, Chairman, Congressman Rohrabacher. I'm extremely pleased to be here to testify and I was thinking this may be the first time I'm testifying after a person had visited a country. Usually, we have hearings before to put pressure but you held one.

But it's one of the realities of the occasion that after the visit we are having a hearing. That says it all about President Obama's human rights commitment and the way they negotiate human rights issues along with other issues.

I also want to make sure that my written testimony is entered into the record.

Mr. SMITH. Without objection, so ordered.

Mr. KUMAR. Thank you.

Amnesty International has been working on human rights in Vietnam and other countries but in Vietnam for more than three, four decades. Things have never improved.

It's improved sometimes when U.S. Presidents and others pushed and opened up a little bit. So the situation did not improve even when President Obama was about to visit.

There were two things that happened before his visit. One is the annual human rights dialogue that took place between Vietnam and the U.S. No improvement at all.

This became more of a annual exercise for the sake of having a dialogue. We thought something would happen because President Obama is about to visit.

So then just before President Obama visited, for 2 weeks before, Assistant Secretary Malinowski and from the White House senior officials were there negotiating tried to get some results. Nothing except Father Ly, who was just released a couple of weeks before his due date.

Then President Obama arrived. The administration, I will say, has misguided us before—they told us, we asked specifically, there are reports that the arms embargo will be lifted and they gave an indication that no, that's not the case.

Even though Amnesty International did not take a position, we want to know what's going on because the reports are coming.

Whether that was an intentional way of silencing us or whatever the reason, the very senior officials told us don't worry, no, no, no, we will consult you and all the rest of it.

And everyone knew that the trade agreement, TPP, was one of the main reasons—one of President Obama's legacy. He wanted to keep that as a legacy.

So these two issues were there. He went in, obviously being nice to Vietnam is to get them on board for TPP and also to everyone's surprise he announced that the arms embargo would be lifted. Okay, you have done all these things. You have given more than enough Vietnamese may have expected. But what in return you got was a slap in your face. In a nutshell, that is what happened.

While he was there, people were arrested for peacefully protesting. People were held incommunicado house arrest, tortured. And it is very rarely defined, when a U.S. President is visiting a country, a host country pretty much treats someone who this particular President, or any U.S. President, is caring and supports his people without abusing them.

That raises a serious question about how Vietnamese authorities look at President Obama's administration and also the U.S. for President Obama, as mentioned earlier, it is a slap in the face. He should have walked out.

He should have said, I am leaving until you release these folks. He didn't do it. He was there enjoying all the parties and whatever he wanted to do, getting all the goodies.

So it is disappointing. The big challenge the U.S. Government in the future will face is President Obama has lowered the bar so low that it will be very difficult for the next President whoever it may be to raise it.

So that is a big challenge that the next administration should focus and to be mindful. Otherwise, it is going to be repeated. It is not only Vietnam. Other countries will feel the same way. Okay, we can push them and they will bend over backwards if we give a trade agreement and whatever the regional stability issues.

The issues in Vietnam nearly everyone else said so I don't want to repeat. But it's really disturbing. Numerous people have been arrested. Prisoners of conscience have been imprisoned, tortured, died in custody.

The list goes on. No institution is free there. Everything is under the control of the government, even the judiciary.

So, no independent judiciary. No independent media. No independent institutions. Nothing is there. It is the government that controls everything and decides everything and lock people up—anyone who raises any voice.

So as I mentioned earlier, President Obama's trip has sent an extremely negative impression to people of Vietnam and to people around the world that you can—you don't have to take the U.S. seriously when it comes to human rights.

Thank you very much, Chairman, for inviting me and looking forward to the questions.

[The prepared statement of Mr. Kumar follows:]

President Obama's Visit to Vietnam: A Missed Opportunity to Advance Human Rights?

Amnesty International Testimony

Before:

Committee on Foreign Affairs
Subcommittee on Africa, Global Health, Global Human Rights, and
International Organizations
U.S. House of Representatives

Testimony by:

T. Kumar
International Advocacy Director

Amnesty International, USA

June 22, 2016

Thank you Mr. Chairman and members of the Committee for holding this hearing and for inviting Amnesty International to testify.

Amnesty International has been working on Vietnam for several decades and has documented serious human rights violations committed by the Vietnamese government. Due to the serious nature of the violations, the U.S. initiated an annual human rights dialogue in order to improve human rights conditions there.

In Vietnam, severe restrictions on the rights to freedom of expression, association and peaceful assembly continued. The media and the judiciary, as well as political and religious institutions, remained under state control. <u>At least 82 prisoners of conscience remain imprisoned in harsh conditions after unfair trials.</u> They included bloggers, labor and land rights activists, political activists, religious followers, members of ethnic groups and advocates for human rights and social justice.

Activists were convicted in new trials. The authorities attempted to prevent the activities of independent civil society groups through harassment, surveillance and restrictions on freedom of movement. A reduction in criminal prosecutions of bloggers and activists coincided with an increase in harassment, short-term arbitrary detentions and physical attacks by security officers. Scores of Montagnard asylum-seekers fled to Cambodia and Thailand between October 2014 and December 2015. The death penalty was retained.

President Obama's visit

President Obama's visit to Vietnam has raised serious questions about the effectiveness of President Obama's human rights policy and about whether Vietnamese authorities take the United States seriously when it comes to human rights issues.

Not only did the Vietnamese government not release any prisoners of conscience beyond Father Ly, it also went ahead with its assault on freedom of expression and peaceful assembly by arresting six peaceful activists and orchestrating a campaign of intimidation and harassment against dozens more during President Obama's visit.

In addition to arrests, dozens of activists have complained that they are being prevented from leaving their homes by uniformed and plain clothes officers. The authorities' crackdown has included the banning of BBC journalists, and the blocking of social media sites including Facebook and Instagram.

Even though President Obama has missed the opportunity to secure the release of prisoners of conscience, in the remaining six months in office he can use his office to secure the release of prisoners of conscience still in custody.

Since President Obama will leave office in six months' time, we hope the new incoming President will reevaluate U.S. – Vietnam human rights policy and make human rights one of the pillars of interaction with the Vietnamese government, along with other interests.

KEY HUMAN RIGHTS CONCERNS

BACKGROUND

A major legislative reform program continued. Several key laws were under review or being drafted. The amended Civil Code, the Penal Code, the Law on Custody and Detention and the Criminal Procedure Code were approved by the end of the year, but a Law on Associations, a Law on Demonstrations, and a Law on Belief and Religion were not finalized. Comments from the general public were solicited. Independent civil society groups raised concerns that some of the laws were not in accordance with Viet Nam's international obligations, including those set out in the International Covenant on Civil and Political Rights, which Viet Nam has ratified.

The UN Convention against Torture entered into force in February, but the needed wide-ranging legal reforms for compliance were still pending.

More than 18,000 prisoners were released to mark the 70th anniversary of National Day in September; no prisoners of conscience were included.

Scores of Montagnard asylum-seekers from the Central Highlands fled to Cambodia and Thailand between October 2014 and December 2015, mostly alleging religious persecution and harassment. Dozens were forcibly returned to Viet Nam from Cambodia, with others voluntarily returning after the Cambodian authorities refused to register them and process their asylum claims. Their fate on return was not known.

REPRESSION OF DISSENT

Members of independent activist groups attempting to exercise their rights to freedom of expression, association and peaceful assembly faced regular harassment, including surveillance, restrictions on movement, arbitrary short-term detention and physical attacks by police and unidentified men suspected of working in collusion with security forces. Dozens of activists were attacked, many of them before or after visiting released prisoners and victims of human rights violations, or when attending events or meetings.

In July, security forces harassed and intimidated peaceful activists attempting to participate in hunger strikes in four major cities in solidarity with prisoners of conscience. The action was organized by the "We Are One" campaign, launched in March together with a letter to the UN Human Rights Council on the human rights situation in Viet Nam, signed by 27 local civil society organizations and 122 individuals.

The authorities continued to use vaguely worded offenses to charge and convict peaceful activists, mainly through Article 258 (abusing democratic freedoms to infringe upon the interests of the state, the legitimate rights and interests of organizations and/or citizens) of the 1999 Penal Code. Three pro-democracy activists arrested in May 2014 while monitoring anti-China protests were sentenced in February to between 12 and 18 months' imprisonment under Article 258 in Đồng Nai province.

Prominent human rights lawyer and former prisoner of conscience Nguyễn Văn Đài and his colleague, Lê Thu Hà, were arrested in December on charges of "conducting propaganda" against the state under Article 88 of the Penal Code. The arrest took place several days after Nguyễn Văn Đài and three colleagues were brutally assaulted by 20 men in plain clothes shortly after delivering human rights training in Nghệ An province. Blogger Nguyễn Hữu Vinh and his associate Nguyễn Thị Minh Thúy remained held in pre-trial detention since their arrest in May 2014. They were charged under Article 258 of the Penal Code in February in connection with the blogs Dân Quyền (Citizens' Rights) and Chép sử Việt (Writing Vietnam's History), both critical of government policies and officials and since closed down.

They were tried in March 2016 and sentenced to five and three years' imprisonment respectively. Prominent blogger and journalist Tạ Phong Tần was released in September and flown immediately into effective exile in the USA. She had served four years of a 10-year prison term on charges of "conducting propaganda" against the state. Reports of repression of religious activities outside state-approved churches continued, including against Hoa Hao Buddhists, Catholic practitioners and Christian ethnic minorities.

FREEDOM OF MOVEMENT

While the number of arrests and prosecutions against human rights defenders and government critics decreased from previous years, physical attacks and restrictions on movement increased. Several activists were confined to their homes. Some of those wishing to travel overseas to attend human rights-related events had their passports confiscated; several others who managed to leave were arrested and interrogated by the police on their return.

Trần Thị Nga, a member of the independent Vietnamese Women for Human Rights group was arrested by security officers on her way to meet a foreign delegation to the Inter-Parliamentary Union Assembly in the capital Ha Noi in March. Security officers beat her while she was being forcibly driven back to her home in Hà Nam province with her two young children.

DEATHS IN CUSTODY

In March, the National Assembly questioned the credibility of a Ministry of Public Security announcement that of 226 deaths in police custody between October 2011 and September 2014, most were caused by illness or suicide. During 2015 at least seven deaths in custody were reported with suspicions of possible police torture or other ill-treatment.

DEATH PENALTY

The National Assembly approved the reduction in the number of capital offences from 22 to 15, as well as abolition for alleged offenders aged 75 and over. Death sentences for drug-related offences continued to be imposed. Although official statistics remained classified as a state secret, the Justice Minister was reported to have said in October that 684 prisoners were on death row. At least 45 death sentences were reported in the media. In January, the Supreme People's Procuracy was tasked with reviewing 16 death penalty cases in which the defendants alleged they had been tortured during police interrogation. In October, Lê Văn Mạnh's execution was postponed for further investigation. He alleged he was tortured in police custody.

RECENT TRIALS

On 23 March 2016, blogger Nguyễn Hữu Vinh and his associate Nguyễn Thị Minh Thúy were tried, convicted and sentenced to five and three years' imprisonment respectively. They were charged under Article 258 of the Penal Code in February in connection with the blogs Dân Quyền (Citizens' Rights) and Chép sử Việt (Writing Vietnam's History), both critical of government policies and officials and since closed down.

Three women activists were also tried on 30 March. Ngô Thị Minh Ước, Nguyễn Thị Trí, and Nguyễn Thị Bé Hai were sentenced to between three and four years' imprisonment under Article 88 of the Penal Code for protesting about land grabs outside the US Embassy in July 2014.

Nguyễn Ngọc Già, another blogger whose real name is Nguyễn Đình Ngọc, was tried on 30 March and sentenced to four years' imprisonment under Article 88 of the Penal Code. He had advocated for freedom of expression and other human rights, and wrote about corruption and injustice.

RECENT PROTESTS

In May 2016, The Vietnamese authorities cracked down heavily in response to a series of demonstrations taking place throughout the country, organized following an ecological catastrophe that has decimated the nation's fish stocks. Wide-ranging police measures to prevent and punish participation in demonstrations resulted in a range of human rights violations including torture and other cruel, inhuman or degrading treatment and punishment, as well as violations of the rights to peaceful assembly and freedom of movement. Dozens were arrested during the course of protests held on 1, 8 and 15 May. While all have since been released, their treatment raised serious concerns over the authorities' response to peaceful protest.

RECENT ARRESTS

Can Thi Theu, a well-known land rights activist, was arrested on 10 June 2016 and detained under Article 245 of the 1999 Penal Code for "causing public disorder". She could be imprisoned for up to seven years if tried and convicted. She has previously been imprisoned and subject to harassment for her peaceful activism.

Indefinite House Arrest

THICH QUANG DO, UNDER INDEFINITE DE FACTO HOUSE ARREST

The Most Venerable Thich Quang Do, 87, is the Patriarch of the banned Unified Buddhist Church of Viet Nam (UBCV). He is a leading advocate of religious freedom, human rights and democracy. He is confined to the Thanh Minh Zen monastery in Ho Chi Minh City as a prisoner of conscience. He has protested peacefully against repressive government policies in Viet Nam since the 1950s and has spent almost three decades either in prison, detained without trial or under house arrest in "internal

The UBCV was founded in 1964, but has been banned since 1975. Its members have come under varying degrees of repression for their peaceful activities, including imprisonment for terms of eight years or more, arbitrary detention and house arrest. They have also been subjected to restrictions on movement and harassment to prevent them from exercising their rights to freedom of expression, association and peaceful assembly, including the right to freedom of belief or religion.

Thich Quang Do's current detention under house arrest began almost 13 years ago in October 2003 while he was returning to Ho Chi Minh City from a UBCV meeting in another province. Security officials told him that he had been placed in administrative detention for an indefinite period; he was not told why he had been arrested, or whether he had been charged with any offence. Security officials keep him under constant surveillance and monitor his phone calls. Police officials have harassed and turned away some overseas visitors, including officials from other countries.

Thich Quang Do suffers from diabetes and high blood pressure. He has won worldwide recognition for his peaceful activism and calls for religious and political freedom, and human rights in Viet Nam. He has been nominated nine times for the Nobel Peace Prize, most recently in 2008, and was the recipient of both the Norwegian Rafto Prize and the World Movement for Democracy "Democracy Courage Tribute" in 2006. He had been honored by the Czech People in Need Foundation and received the 2001 Hellman-Hammet Award for persecuted writers.

In November 2015, Amnesty International co-sponsored an Open Letter to President Obama, calling on him to press Viet Nam for the release of Thich Quang Do. The letter was endorsed by academics, legislators, artists, religious leaders, members of international institutions and civil society organizations worldwide.

I also would like to highlight Amnesty International's Chapter's activities on this case. For example, Amnesty International's Chapter 56 in Lexington, Massachusetts have been working on the case since 2002, including Thich Quang Do's predecessor Thich Huyen Quang. During that time they have written thousands of letter to Vietnamese officials, circulated petitions with hundreds of signatures of Amnesty International members throughout the US, published letters to the editor on behalf of our prisoner in the Boston Globe, organized write-in's in our local community, worked closely with other Amnesty International groups in Canada, Sweden and other countries, contacted chief executive offices of major US corporations doing business in Vietnam, initiated a "dear colleague" from members of the MA congressional delegation to Pres Obama on his recent visit to Vietnam.

PRISONERS OF CONSCIENCE

At least 82 prisoners of conscience remained in detention. The majority were convicted under vaguely worded national security provisions of the Penal Code: Article 79 ("overthrowing" the state) or Article 88 ("conducting propaganda").

At least 17 were released after completing their prison sentences but remained under house arrest for specified periods. Thích Quảng Độ, head of the banned Unified Buddhist Church of Vietnam, spent his 12th year under de facto house arrest. Some prisoners were pressed to "confess" to charges in exchange for a reduction in sentence.

Conditions of detention and treatment of prisoners of conscience continued to be harsh. This included lack of physical exercise; verbal and physical attacks; prolonged detention in hot cells with little natural light; denial of sanitary equipment; frequent prison transfers; and detention far from homes and families, making family visits difficult.

Several undertook hunger strikes in protest at the use of solitary confinement and abusive treatment of prisoners, including Tạ Phong Tần (see above); Nguyễn Đặng Minh Mẫn, serving an eight-year sentence; and Đinh Nguyên Kha, serving a four-year sentence. Nguyễn Văn Duyệt, a Catholic social activist serving a three-and-a-half-year sentence, protested at being denied a Bible; and social justice activist Hồ Thị Bích Khương, serving a five-year sentence, protested when she was not allowed to take personal belongings when transferred to another prison.

Here are some of the names of Prisoners of Conscience

BÙI THỊ MINH HẰNG (F) SENTENCED TO THREE YEARS IMPRISONMENT

Bùi Thị Minh Hằng, is a prominent land rights activist who is also known for participating in demonstrations against China's controversial territorial claims in the South China Sea and related policies of the Vietnamese government. She is serving a three-year sentence under Article 245 of the Penal Code for creating "serious obstruction to traffic", and is being denied medical treatment. She was arrested on 11 February 2014 on her way to visit human rights lawyer Nguyễn Bắc Truyển. Hằng was held incommunicado until the end of March 2014 when she was finally allowed to meet a lawyer and member of her family. During that time, she embarked on a hunger strike in protest. Bùi Thị Minh Hằng was held in Đồng Tháp prison until her trial on 26 August 2014.

After her trial, Bùi Thị Minh Hằng was transferred to Gia Trung prison in Gia Lai province, some 1,000 km from her family, making visits very difficult. She has developed a range of medical problems: a painful stomach ulcer, low blood pressure, joint pain, frequent severe headaches and occasional blackouts. Despite repeated requests, she has received no medical treatment from independent doctors. The prison authorities also meted out punitive treatment when she advocated for better treatment of prisoners, allowing harassment by fellow prisoners, denying family visits and communication. She is due for release in 2017.

ĐẶNG XUÂN DIỆU (M) SENTENCED TO 13 YEARS IMPRISONMENT, FIVE YEARS HOUSE ARREST

Đặng Xuân Diệu, a Catholic, is an engineer, blogger and social activist, who was arrested in July 2011, and sentenced in January 2013 under Article 79 of the Penal Code to 13 years' imprisonment with five years' house arrest on release. He was accused of connections to an overseas based group campaigning for democracy in Viet Nam. He submitted numerous complaints to the authorities, denying his guilt and claiming his trial was unfair.

Details emerged of the treatment of Đặng Xuân Diệu following the release in October 2014 of a prisoner who was held in an adjacent cell in Prison No 5, Thanh Hóa province. According to his account, Đặng Xuân Diệu had variously been held in solitary confinement for prolonged periods, beaten by prison guards, shackled in a cell with a prisoner who beat him, forced to drink unclean water, denied water for washing, a blanket and mosquito net, and lived in unsanitary conditions with no toilet in the cell. He reported that Đặng Xuân Diệu had gone on several hunger strikes in protest of his treatment and was subsequently moved to a different prison - Xuyên Mộc, in Bà Rịa-Vũng Tàu province in the south. He is not due for release until 2024.

ĐOÀN HUY CHƯƠNG (M) SENTENCED TO SEVEN YEARS' IMPRISONMENT; NGUYỄN HOÀNG QUỐC HÙNG (M) SENTENCED TO NINE YEARS' IMPRISONMENT

Đoàn Huy Chương, a former prisoner of conscience, and Nguyễn Hoàng Quốc Hùng are labor organizers and members of the independent United Workers-Farmers Organization arrested in February 2010. They have both stated that they were beaten during pre-trial detention in order to make them "confess" to the charges against them. They were tried by a court in Tra Vinh province in October 2010 and sentenced to seven and nine years' imprisonment, respectively, under Article 89 of the Penal Code for "disrupting security". They handed out advice leaflets at a shoe factory in Tra Vinh where the workers were protesting their pay and working conditions. Đoàn Huy Chương is detained at Z30A prison, Xuân Lộc in Đồng Nai province; Nguyễn Hoàng Quốc Hùng is in Xuyên Mộc prison, Bà Rịa-Vũng Tàu province, where he is said to have been put in solitary confinement for protesting the installation of a camera in his cell. In March 2016, he took part in a 13-day hunger strike with four other prisoners of conscience in protest at treatment and conditions in Xuyên Mộc.

LÊ THANH TÙNG (M) IN PRE-TRIAL DETENTION

Lê Thanh Tùng, a former prisoner of conscience, journalist and member of the pro-democracy group Bloc 8406, was arrested around 14 or 15 December 2015 in Gia Lai province. His house in Ha Noi was searched by police on 24 December 2015, who removed personal items. He was released in June 2015, six months before completing a four-year prison term imposed in August 2012 under Article 88 of the Penal Code. Since his release he is reported to have continued to advocate for democracy and to be part of the same group formed by another former prisoner of conscience, Trần Anh Kim, who has also been arrested (see below). He is reported to have been moved to Thái Bình province, but his family has not been officially informed of his whereabouts.

NGUYỄN VĂN ĐÀI (M); LÊ THU HÀ (F) IN PRE-TRIAL DETENTION

Human rights lawyer Nguyễn Văn Đài, and his Brotherhood for Democracy colleague Lê Thu Hà were arrested on 16 December 2015. They are both charged under Article 88 of the Penal Code and have been held incommunicado since then, with their families and lawyers denied access to them. They are currently held in B14 Detention Centre, Ha Noi. Activists who tried to visit them a few days after their arrests were denied access, and Nguyễn Văn Đài's wife has complained that her efforts to pass on warm clothing and supplies for him were obstructed. In February 2016, before the Lunar New Year holiday, prison authorities refused to allow Nguyễn Văn Đài to receive a Bible and legal magazines brought by his wife. She says that she does not know whether he currently needs medicine for his Hepatitis B and, if so, whether that medicine is being provided by the prison authorities.

SIU WIU (M) SENTENCED TO 10 YEARS' IMPRISONMENT

Siu Wiu is a Montagnard Christian activist from the Central Highlands and one of the leaders of a demonstration in Gia Lai province in April 2008 that called for religious freedom and release of Montagnard prisoners of conscience. According to his indictment, under the direction of Montagnard exiles abroad, Siu Wiu incited people to prepare banners with "reactionary anti-government content". In January 2009, he was sentenced to 10 years in prison under Penal Code Article 89, disrupting security. While imprisoned at Nam Hà Prison he spent six months in solitary confinement before being transferred to Phú Sơn 4 Prison in Tây Nguyên province, even farther away from his family in Gia Lai. During pre-trial detention, police tortured him for more than two months during interrogation sessions. Among the torture tactics they employed was to hang him upside down and beat him with wooden batons.

VENERABLE THACH THUOL (M) SENTENCED TO SIX YEARS' IMPRISONMENT

Venerable Thach Thuol is a Khmer Krom Buddhist monk and deputy abbot of Serei Ta Sek Temple in Sóc Trăng province. In March 2013 local authorities and Buddhist officials ordered Thach Thuol and two other Khmer Krom monks to defrock or face imprisonment, alleging that the three were spreading "fabricated information" abroad about rights violations in Vietnam, through interviews with foreign media and contact with the Khmer Krom Federation, a US-based advocacy group. On May 18, 2013, police arrested, detained and tortured one of Thach Thuol's fellow monks in Sóc Trăng. That same day, more than 100 police surrounded Thach Thuol's temple in an effort to arrest and defrock him. After making an impassioned video appeal that was posted online, in which he expressed fears that he too would be tortured, he attempted to flee Vietnam to seek political asylum. On May 20, 2013 police arrested him at the Vietnam-Cambodia border. During pre-trial detention, police beat Thach Thuol during interrogation sessions. He refused to confess to any crimes and continued to assert his innocence at his trial in September 2013. He was sentenced to six years' imprisonment under Article 91, fleeing abroad to oppose the people's administration, and is currently serving his sentence at Xuân Lộc Prison in Đồng Nai Province.

TRẦN ANH KIM (M) IN PRE-TRIAL DETENTION

Trần Anh Kim is a former prisoner of conscience, army officer and writer. He was arrested in September 2015 for investigation under Article 79 of the Penal Code. It is believed to be in connection with a group that he was about to launch named "Raising the flag of democracy" (Lực Lượng Quốc Dân Dựng Cờ Dân Chủ). Trần Anh Kim, a supporter of Bloc 8406, was previously sentenced to five and a half years' imprisonment with three years' house arrest on release in December 2009 for his peaceful activities protesting against injustice and government corruption; he was released in January 2015 and re-arrested eight months later. Following his arrest, he was initially believed held in Thái Bình province, but there are unconfirmed reports he has been moved to B14 prison in Ha Noi.

TRẦN HUỲNH DUY THỨC (M) SENTENCED TO 16 YEARS' IMPRISONMENT AND FIVE YEARS' HOUSE ARREST

Trần Huỳnh Duy Thức declared during his trial that he was tortured in detention to force him to confess. He is an entrepreneur, blogger and human rights defender who was arrested in May 2009. He was initially accused of "theft of telephone wires" before being charged under Article 88 for "conducting propaganda" against the state. However, he was tried by Ho Chi Minh City People's Court on 20 January 2010 under Article 79 of the Penal Code and sentenced to 16 years' imprisonment with five years' house arrest on release. According to witnesses, the judges deliberated for only 15 minutes before returning with the judgment, which took 45 minutes to read, indicating it had been prepared in advance of the hearing. After the trial Trần Huỳnh Duy Thức was transferred to Xuân Lộc, Đồng Nai province. In June 2013 he was moved to Xuyên Mộc Prison, Bà Rịa-Vũng Tàu province, following a protest at harsh treatment by criminal prisoners in one section of Xuân Lộc. His family were not informed of the transfer until they arrived at Xuân Lộc to visit him. In March 2016, he took part in the hunger strike described above together with Nguyễn Hoàng Quốc Hùng and three others. He was moved again in May 2016 from Xuyên Mộc prison camp to Prison No 6 in Nghệ An province. The transfer was possibly connected with his refusal to agree to be relocated to the United States as a condition for early release. He began a hunger-strike beginning 24 May 2016 to demand rule of law and a referendum on Viet Nam's political system. He is not due for release until 2025.

TRẦN THỊ THÚY (F) SENTENCED TO EIGHT YEARS' IMPRISONMENT

Trần Thị Thúy is a Hoa Hao Buddhist and land rights activist arrested in August 2010 who is serving an eight-year sentence after being convicted under Article 79 of the Penal Code by Bến Tre Provincial People's Court on 30 May 2011. She and six other land rights activists were accused of having joined or been associated with an overseas based pro-democracy group. Since being detained, Trần Thị Thúy has been denied medical treatment on the grounds that she hasn't "confessed" her crimes. She became ill in April 2015 while she was detained in a facility at Long Khánh town in Đồng Nai Province. A prison doctor diagnosed a tumor in her uterus, but she was not provided with treatment. A prison officer told her to admit her crimes or "die in prison". She has difficulty walking, needing a crutch or help. She also has high blood pressure for which she takes medication. Tran Thi Thuy is in severe physical pain and has told her family that she has felt on the verge of death at several points in recent months. She is currently detained in An Phước Prison, Bình Dương province, which is approximately 900 km, or three days travel from her family. Tran Thi Thuy is due for release in 2018.

Recommendations:

1) Even though President Obama has missed the opportunity to secure the release of prisoners of conscience, in the remaining six months in office he can use his office to secure the release of prisoners of conscience still in custody.

2) We also urge the new incoming President to reevaluate U.S. – Vietnam human rights policy and make human rights one of the pillars of interaction with the Vietnamese government.

Thank you for inviting Amnesty International to testify.

T. Kumar
International Advocacy Director
Amnesty International USA

Email: tkumar@aiusa.org

Mr. SMITH. Mr. Kumar, thank you again for your extraordinary candor. You, for years, no matter what the country that is being highlighted and focused upon, have always given such extremely valuable insights—unvarnished, no matter who is in the White House, Republican or Democrat, and I think that serves, obviously, the victims and the potential victims so extremely well.

And to break this pattern of complicity, in my opinion, that this administration has engaged in with dictatorships, you are right, we need to be still hoping maybe against hope that this administration will find its voice on human rights and stop the rhetorical flourish and be substantive.

I would just say that I have authored a number of laws on human rights, as you know. The international child abduction law—it is called the Goldman Act—the Sean and David Goldman International Child Abduction Prevention and Return Act—that legislation has a report attached to it as well as other aspects to it.

Last year they got it wrong, famously wrong, about Japan and other nations. It was due on April 30th. That report is late. It will probably come as soon as we go into recess when everybody in the House and Senate are out of town. How cynical is that?

The Trafficking Victims Protection Act last year—I am the author of the Trafficking Victims Protection Act and the TIP Report that comes out annually was due at the beginning of the month if not earlier. That has not yet arrived.

Last year, 14 countries were erroneously placed or given passing grades when the TIP office itself thought those 14 countries should have been what we call Tier 3—as you know, egregious violators and gave out inflated grades—in other words, bending the rules, breaking the rules I would suggest—for political reasons and not human rights criteria.

The Reuters news organization did an incisive series of investigative reports that found that country after country, from Cuba to China to Oman—all these countries that should have gotten horrible grades got passing grades through this administration, contrary to what their own TIP office had said they should be given because it was done for political reasons.

So I find it abhorrent in the extreme that the President would go to Vietnam. There is an old saying—thanks, but no thanks. If I were a dissident in Vietnam, I would say, no thanks, Mr. President—please don't come, as well as the other phrase, more harm than good.

You pointed out, Dr. Thang, that many people were arrested and harassed before, then during, and I am sure after as well. These people have suffered beatings and torture, directly attributable to the President's visit.

That is unconscionable. The President should be on that phone. He should have said to the leadership in Vietnam even while there, if you do any more of this then I am out of here—I will make an international incident—I stand with the oppressed, and I said earlier, not with the oppressor and you need to stop it.

I know there are people from the Vietnamese Government in this room. I hope they convey that back to Hanoi. I find it appalling.

If you were in trouble we would be fighting for you, and many people who are in government one day find themselves on the wrong side of the dictatorship and other, and who do they come to? They often come to the democracies including and especially the United States.

A couple questions—I sensed a failure of the White House press corps and of the press corps generally to really rein in and focus on what was happening to the dissidents. There were a few stories—to me, it should have been the main story—that the President goes to Vietnam.

Dissidents, journalists, bloggers, and people fighting for environmental protections were rounded up and tortured. That should have been the story, and yet it seems not to have been.

Rabbi Saperstein testified last week before our subcommittee and I have a great deal of respect for him as the Ambassador-at-Large. But to think that he would meet with Mrs. Hong and she'd be beaten as well as others when he meets with them, that should have been the absolute red line that once crossed all bets were off.

There should be a rescission of the lifting of the arms embargo. The President should do that today. There is nothing precluding him from today saying that arms embargo lifting, it is not going to happen—I am reversing myself because of the egregious human rights abuses being committed.

So if you could maybe touch on the press corps side of it, what we ought to be doing further. We want to get the Frank R. Wolf International Religious Freedom Act out of the Senate.

The Frank R. Wolf International Religious Freedom Act, which had 118 cosponsors including my good friend and colleague Chairman Rohrabacher, passed overwhelmingly. It is sitting in the Senate. My hope is they take it up soon.

The Vietnam Human Rights Act—we are hoping our committee will take it up. I am talking about the full Committee on Foreign Affairs. Remember it passed four times.I21Even if it dies again in the Senate we will back again next year. We have to be as tenacious as the people who are suffering, giving of their blood and of their freedom. We could do no less. So we need to get that enacted as well as others.

Ms. Duong, you talked about how they are using visas denying the ability to travel. Under the International Religious Freedom Act, and Vietnam should have been yesterday, but certainly today, designated as a CPC and when I did press Rabbi Saperstein on that, the Ambassador-at-Large, last week, there are provisions in there to deny visas to those who commit crimes against religious believers and they are done in a targeted and a calibrated way.

Unfortunately, even under the Bush administration, there was one and that was against Modi, now the head of state for India. That tool needs to be used much more aggressively and it seems to me Vietnam should get that CPC designation and the visa ban needs to be imposed on people who hurt Cao Dai or Christians or anyone else.

So on those few questions, then I yield to my friend, Mr. Rohrabacher.

Mr. ROHRABACHER. Pastor Loan, you were ministering to the Montagnard people? When did you leave the central highlands?

Pastor LOAN. May 2014.

Mr. ROHRABACHER. All right. I spent some time there in 1967 in Pleiku or near Pleiku anyway—that little French fort. They have a little French fort over there. I was operating out of there.

Pastor LOAN. I know.

Mr. ROHRABACHER. Okay. We won't go into what's gone on in that fort now. Kind of interesting what they did with it.

But I know that the Montagnards were incredibly brave people, and did they suffer disproportionately after the Americans left? Those Montagnards who had allied with us, did they suffer more than other people in Vietnam?

Pastor LOAN. After the Americans left Vietnam that is when they started torturing the Montagnard people such as the people who joined force with the American force, helping Americans during the Vietnam War. They went hard on them, made them suffer or their family, basically, yes, after the Vietnam War.

Mr. ROHRABACHER. I have often wondered what had happened to some of the people I knew there and let me just note that the Vietnamese people sided with us during the Cold War and we walked away and they suffered because of it. However, we can make up for that, Mr. Chairman, by trying to be a strong voice now in trying to evolve communism out of that repressive system.

(Applause.)

Let me ask, does anyone here believe—well, first of all, in Vietnam now do they still use all these Communist slogans? Do they still use the Communist slogans to control the people?

Does anyone here believe that they really believe in Marxism, Leninism? Do the people running the government actually believe in Marxist-Leninist principles, which is the basis of communism?

My theory is they don't believe in this at all. They are just a bunch of thugs and gangsters and they could not care less about trying to create this new man that doesn't have any of this Communist propaganda that threatened the world for a long time, in fact.

So they don't believe in it. Here they claim, using Communist slogans, yet Mr. Chairman, they are partnering with American businessmen in order to exploit their own people.

Now we have a partnership between the ultimate capitalist and these Vietnamese ''leaders,'' the gangsters who run the country and then they have the gall to say that they are Communist when they are exploiting their own people and they are partnering with our own companies.

Now, I am ashamed of our own companies, the Americans who are willing to use a totalitarian control of a people under the name of communism in order for them to make a profit. We saw that in China as well.

I was very interested in what you were saying about the sermons, that the Communists actually come in and tell you that you have to get approval of your sermon before you are able to give it.

I think that is so alien to Americans they could not imagine that that is happening in any country. How can anybody even imagine that?

Mr. Chairman, I remember Ronald Reagan stated very clearly, he said that one of the biggest problems is that for Americans, who take freedom for granted because freedom is invisible. Freedom is when you don't have someone having to look at your sermon before you give the sermon.

Freedom is when you don't have to get permission to do something before you do it and in dictatorships like in Vietnam that repression is there and the people see it every day.

But Americans don't even know what to look for and that is why hearings like this are very important. And let me just note that it was very poignant, sir. You said that you are not allowed to use the word "freedom."

And let me note, this is—I am sorry for being political here but we have a President of the United States who is unable to use the words "radical Islamic terrorist" and these people know that words have meaning and that is why the regime now, the gangster regime in Vietnam know that words have meaning.

They don't want that powerful word there because freedom also implies responsibility and accountability because you have freedom of the press, which you don't have under this Communist system. And so these things all tie together.

Let us hope that we are a shining light to the world, especially a beacon of hope to people who sided with us when they thought they were going to help us, and thank you again.

I do believe that now is the time for the American people not just come to partnership with this TPP they are talking about.

How could we possibly go along with an agreement that allows these gangsters to possibly be on that commission to decide whether or not we are in compliance with the trade treaty?

It is a total elimination of standards and values for consideration and we should be instead fighting to make sure there are higher standards than just having our businessmen go over there and make a profit from basically labor that is not permitted to organize and from Vietnamese people who are being suppressed and their standard of living is so much lower than elsewhere.

So thank you all very much for testifying today. Thank you, Mr. Chairman, for chairing this hearing.

Mr. SMITH. Thank you, Chair Rohrabacher.

I did ask a few earlier questions and if you could come back to those and maybe add answers to them and this one would be to Mr. Kumar.

The U.N. Special Rapporteur on the freedom of religion or belief, Bielefeldt, has said—regarding Vietnam—that the rights of freedom of religion and belief of such communities are grossly violated—we are talking about independent religious belief communities—in the face of constant surveillance, intimidation, harassment and persecution and, of course, Pastor Loan's church at least has some recognition and yet he has had such terrible experiences.

What possibly might the Special Rapporteur do? Secondly, in your testimony you talk about the U.N. Convention Against Torture, entered into force in February, and you also pointed out that the We Are One campaign launched and in March a letter went to the U.N. Human Rights Council, so another bite of the apple, if you will, of trying to get the U.N. further engaged on human rights there.

There were many signers, 27 local civil society organizations and 122 organizations. Is that bearing any fruit at the U.N. in terms of their reaction to these terrible abuses?

Mr. KUMAR. At the U.N., depending on that day, the Human Rights Council member states that are there, it is having some impact, especially when the special rapporteurs give their reports. So it takes some time.

But there is some movement in that direction and also to the same point, U.S. is not a member at this moment for the last 1 year. It is running to be elected so in November we will know the results. But more than likely the U.S. will get elected.

So once it gets elected, we want U.S. to take the leadership on religious freedom issues in some countries, especially Vietnam.

Mr. SMITH. If the United States leads and leads with transparency and strength and really speaks truth to power and not only affects the dictatorships of the world including the one that's being focused on but also, I would think, the other democracies who might take their lead from that.

But as you said, if we lower that bar so low, it is, like, everyone just doesn't care or cares a lot less than they would have and the dictatorships like China, North Korea, Iran, and Cuba, look at that and say, they have abandoned human rights—it is all talk—it is all rhetoric.

And I am wondering, when Raul Castro said to the President or said in that meeting, give me the list of prisoners and I will release them, he should have said, here is the list.

He was sitting right there. The State Department has a list. We have a list. We have made a trip down to the Embassy of Cuba several weeks ago trying to get a visa. I want to go. I want to give a list to Raul Castro.

I was told by the Ambassador here in Washington to the United States from Cuba that there are certain parameters that would have to be followed about who I could meet with in terms of the dissident community. And I said do other congressional delegations do that and he said yes.

So they are all pre-screened. Only certain people can be spoken with, or to, in an orchestration of a Potemkin village and they come back glowing about how great things are in Cuba. Well, we see this happening again and again. So that whole idea of human rights leadership—if you would like to answer that.

Let me also ask you, Pastor Loan, you talked about Deacon Ngai being beaten to death. You might give us some additional details about that.

I know it is very painful. But just so we know what happened in that incident, you know, so we have it fully on the record in terms of that brutality. But maybe you could start, Dr. Thang, first.

Pastor LOAN. Deacon Hoang Van Ngai was peaceful. He was a deacon and one day he went to his farm and they went to his farm and get them—beat them there and brought them to their office, their jail, and just tortured him and beat him to death.

After that the girl—the authority did not let anybody see the body of the deacon and said that he died not because of torture but because he wanted to kill himself, that Deacon Ngai wanted to kill himself and did something to himself. That is why he died. It's not them.

And they told me not to say a word about it and threatened my life if I did say something against them that testified that they were the one that beat Deacon Ngai to death and tortured him.

Mr. THANG. Mr. Chairman, I am very knowledgeable about that case. In 2013, Deacon Hoang Van Ngai, a Hmong Christian, who—and whose family were relocated from the northern part of Vietnam, the mountainous part of Vietnam, all the way down to the central part of Vietnam in order to escape persecution in the north.

But he didn't fare any better. He and his brother were captured. Actually, they captured—the police captured their wives first and held them hostage. So Mr. Ngai and the brother had to report themselves to the police in order to set free their wives.

And during detention the police tortured him, forcing him to renounce his faith and he refused repeatedly and he got tortured repeatedly until he died. And then a few months later the entire family—actually, his extended family wrote a petition to the government requesting investigation into his death.

Then his cousin, Hoang Van Sang, living in the north, all the way in the north, got arrested by the police, taken into police custody for 10 days.

After 10 days of detention the police delivered his corpse to his family and told the family that if anyone there should speak out about his death, this is the fate that they would suffer.

And therefore about ten families of Mr. Ngai among his cousins and brothers had to escape to Thailand and our team in Thailand helped them.

Fortunately, a number of them have already been recognized as refugees. And one thing I can say is that in 2014 it was Boat People SOS in conjunction with Christian Solidarity Worldwide, CSW, we broke the news about his death and not Pastor Rmah Loan at all.

But that pointed to a very disturbing trend here. The perpetrators of torture have been treated with impunity in Vietnam while those who reported or believed to have reported torture and human rights abuses are being persecuted and threatened with incarceration, imprisonment, or even death.

So, clearly, Vietnam is not intent on implementing the Convention Against Torture and that kind of policy will only encourage more violence and more torture, and this really is pointing out that our Government hasn't made public condemnation against that kind of practice.

Mr. SMITH. With regards to CPC designation Ambassador Saperstein made very clear and they have always had this authority that such a designation can be made at any time.

It doesn't have to wait for an annual report. When the information on the ground merits it a designation, either improvement or a downgrade—in other words, a CPC designation, can be made.

My question would be in your view should Vietnam receive such a designation, especially in light of Ambassador Saperstein's visit and Mrs. Hong's brutal beating, simply for meeting with the Ambassador-at-Large for international religious freedom.

If that isn't an outrage that is like a tip of the iceberg for all the rest of the cruelty meted out by the Vietnamese I don't know what is.

But your thoughts on that?

Mr. THANG. Mr. Chairman, clearly, it is systematic because that is the law. There is a system. It occurs everywhere, not just in one place—repeatedly, not just one time.

It is egregious. Torture is egregious. Forced renouncement of faith is egregious. Imprisonment is egregious. And it is ongoing. So if we just go by the books, clearly, Vietnam should be designated as CPC, no doubt about that.

I would like to point out one other thing about the U.N. Special Rapporteur on freedom of religion or belief. Last year in September, we organized the first conference on freedom of religion or belief in Southeast Asia and we held it in Bangkok in late September. A number of Cao Dai religious leaders and dignitaries came to that conference to meet with the U.N. Special Rapporteur.

And when they returned to Vietnam they were placed under the visa travel ban, and that's what Ms. Duong just mentioned. So that is very outrageous.

There is an agreement between the Vietnamese Government and the U.N. Human Rights Council. That is, people who talk, who report, who speak to or who make reports to the U.N. Special Rapporteur should not be mistreated or punished.

Mr. SMITH. I will just conclude. Pastor Loan, when you talked about and testified about how the government controls the words that can be used it reminds me of—there was a National Geographic documentary about this eye doctor who went to Pyongyang and was actually helping people with cataracts and other eye problems and many went from being almost blind to being able to see.

Kim Jong Il was the dictator then and his picture was in this mass meeting room where everybody gathered to thank the doctor, and the thanks to the doctor was slim to almost none and their praise and worship of the dictator just eclipsed all else.

It was the government—the cult of personality—and obviously when you have an insecurity on the part of a government like Vietnam where they have to have the thank yous first to them, then to God and anyone else, and all the other wordsmithing that they impose upon even those that are recognized churches it just shows a gross insecurity on the part of that government.

A psychiatrist could have a field day with that, it would seem to me. Dr. Thang, did you want to comment on it?

Mr. THANG. Just about that, I would like to remind everyone here that what is happening with Pastor Rmah Loan's church is actually about a church that has been legally recognized by the Government of Vietnam.

His church is probably the largest Christian church in central highlands, and if there is a Department of State delegation or USCIRF delegation or Member of Congress visiting Vietnam, they most likely would be invited to go to that church to showcase how much freedom of religion there is in Vietnam.

And yet, behind closed doors, that is what is happening. A member of that church—a key member of that church—that is Deacon Hoang Van Ngai—was tortured to death because he refused to renounce his faith and then his pastor was prohibited from making any mention about his death, and then family members have been tracked down and threatened to the point they had to flee their home villages.

And now the pastor is in the U.S. fearing persecution or even imprisonment and death upon return to Vietnam. So that is how a state-sanctioned church is being treated, let alone unrecognized independent religious communities just like the Cao Dai group here that she's represented.

Mr. SMITH. Before I ask you if you have anything final you would like to say, I would like to recognize in the audience two very distinguished persons.

First, Joseph Rees, Ambassador Rees, our first Ambassador to East Timor, or Timor-Leste, who also served many years ago as chief of staff and chief counsel for the International Operations and Human Rights Subcommittee.

In fact, when we were doing many of the initiatives to try to rescue those people who were going to be sent back during the Comprehensive Plan of Action, working with Dr. Thang, Joseph played a pivotal role in ensuring that those 20,000-plus people came here as well as other things.

Also, Anh ''Joseph'' Cao is here as well, a former Congressman and good friend, first Vietnamese-American Congressman, and was a great leader when he was here. We miss him, but it is great to see him and I know he works alongside Boat People SOS as well.

Would any of you like to say anything before we conclude?

Pastor LOAN. I know for sure if I return back to Vietnam there will be punishment for me for sure. So I would like to ask to stay here.

Mr. SMITH. Thank you.

Pastor LOAN. Would you help me get that? Thank you for your time.

Mr. SMITH. Thank you. The hearing is adjourned, and I thank you again.

[Whereupon, at 3:31 p.m., the subcommittee was adjourned.]

APPENDIX

SUBCOMMITTEE HEARING NOTICE
COMMITTEE ON FOREIGN AFFAIRS
U.S. HOUSE OF REPRESENTATIVES
WASHINGTON, DC 20515-6128

Subcommittee on Africa, Global Health, Global Human Rights, and International Organizations
Christopher H. Smith (R-NJ), Chairman

June 22, 2016

TO: MEMBERS OF THE COMMITTEE ON FOREIGN AFFAIRS

You are respectfully requested to attend an OPEN hearing of the Committee on Foreign Affairs, to be held by the Subcommittee on Africa, Global Health, Global Human Rights, and International Organizations in Room 2200 of the Rayburn House Office Building (and available live on the Committee website at http://www.ForeignAffairs.house.gov):

DATE: Wednesday, June 22, 2016

TIME: 2:00 p.m.

SUBJECT: The President's Visit to Vietnam: A Missed Opportunity to Advance Human Rights

WITNESSES: Pastor Rmah Loan
(Former Head, Southern Evangelical Church of Vietnam - Dak Nong Province)

Ms. Katie Duong
Overseas Representative
Popular Bloc of Cao Dai Religion

Nguyen Dinh Thang, Ph.D.
President and Chief Executive Officer
Boat People SOS

Mr. T. Kumar
Director of International Advocacy
Amnesty International

By Direction of the Chairman

The Committee on Foreign Affairs seeks to make its facilities accessible to persons with disabilities. If you are in need of special accommodations, please call 202/225-5021 at least four business days in advance of the event, whenever practicable. Questions with regard to special accommodations in general (including availability of Committee materials in alternative formats and assistive listening devices) may be directed to the Committee.

COMMITTEE ON FOREIGN AFFAIRS

MINUTES OF SUBCOMMITTEE ON _Africa, Global Health, Global Human Rights, and International Organizations_ HEARING

Day __Wednesday__ Date_____ _June 22, 2016_ ____Room _2200 Rayburn HOB_

Starting Time __2:01 p.m.__ Ending Time __3:31 p.m.__

Recesses | _0_ | (____to____) (____to____) (____to____) (____to____) (____to____) (____to____)

Presiding Member(s)

Rep. Chris Smith

Check all of the following that apply:

Open Session ☑
Executive (closed) Session ☐
Televised ☑

Electronically Recorded (taped) ☑
Stenographic Record ☑

TITLE OF HEARING:

The President's Visit to Vietnam: A Missed Opportunity to Advance Human Rights

SUBCOMMITTEE MEMBERS PRESENT:

Rep. Dan Donovan

NON-SUBCOMMITTEE MEMBERS PRESENT: _(Mark with an * if they are not members of full committee.)_

Rep. Dana Rohrabacher

HEARING WITNESSES: Same as meeting notice attached? Yes ☑ No ☐
(If "no", please list below and include title, agency, department, or organization.)

STATEMENTS FOR THE RECORD: _(List any statements submitted for the record.)_

Statement of Ms. Jackie Bong Wright, submitted by Rep. Smith

TIME SCHEDULED TO RECONVENE _____
or
TIME ADJOURNED __3:31 p.m.__

_____
Subcommittee Staff Associate

MATERIAL SUBMITTED FOR THE RECORD BY THE HONORABLE CHRISTOPHER H. SMITH, A REPRESENTATIVE IN CONGRESS FROM THE STATE OF NEW JERSEY, AND CHAIRMAN, SUBCOMMITTEE ON AFRICA, GLOBAL HEALTH, GLOBAL HUMAN RIGHTS, AND INTERNATIONAL ORGANIZATIONS

Two Vietnamese Labor Activists In Jail
By Jackie Bong Wright – June 22, 2016 – Hearing at U.S. Congress

My name is Jackie Bong Wright, a Board member of the Free Viet Labor Federation, or Viet Labor, which was established in 2006, ten years ago. Our mission is to protect the rights of the working class, and organize an Independent Labor Union in Vietnam.

From late January to early February 2010, three young activists - Minh Hanh, 25, Quoc Hung, 29, and Huy Chuong, 25, members of Viet Labor - supported 10,000 workers to organize a strike at the My Phong shoe factory in Tra Vinh province, South Vietnam. They distributed leaflets demanding better pay and better working conditions as well as basic labor rights. They also called for a multi-party system, and a democratic process in Vietnam. They were arrested.

For eight months, they were held incommunicado, without legal counsel; this constituted arbitrary detention, and violated international human rights standards. State authorities not only, barred them from access to lawyers, but also prevented their families from visiting them. Then, in October 2010, Minh Hanh and Huy Chuong, were sentenced to seven years in jail, while Quoc Hung, was sentenced to nine years. The three were convicted of "spreading anti-government propaganda, and disrupting national security, under Article 89 of the Vietnamese Criminal Code."

In 2006, Huy Chuong, a founding member of the "unofficial" United Workers-Farmers Organization, had already been sent in prison for 18 months for defending the rights of impoverished farmers, whose lands had been confiscated by the government. His young son, had epileptic seizures, and his wife was often hospitalized for sicknesses related to exhaustion. During the past six years of his detention, Quoc Hung, on the other hand, has gone on three hunger strikes to protest prisoners' mistreatment by the authorities.

international NGOs as well as Vietnamese Human Rights groups around the world, teamed up to fight for the release of these three young peaceful activists. Freedom Now, along with the law firm Woodley McGillivary, served as international pro bono legal counsel to the trio. As a result, on June 26, 2014, Ms. Minh Hanh was released from prison on medical grounds, after being detained for three and a half years, but her two colleagues, are still serving jail term.

As you may know, under Vietnamese law, workers are prohibited from forming independent unions. All unions must be registered and affiliated with the Vietnam General Confederation of Labor (VGCL), the only official labor entity, which is controlled by the Communist party. These government-affiliated unions can join or participate in international labor bodies, if approved by the VGCL. They have the right to bargain collectively, but the right to strike is severely restricted. Thus, the Communist government continued to repress independent unions.

On behalf of Quoc Hung and Huy Chuong, I'd like to call on the Administration and the U.S. Congress, to demand the immediate release of these two peaceful activists. If Father Ly could be released even before President Obama set foot in Vietnam, the unconditional release of all political prisoners, in particular Quoc Hung and Huy Chuong, should be possible, especially after President Obama's lifting the arms embargo on Vietnam.

Furthermore, as Vietnam has committed to the TPP, the accompanying US-Vietnam Bilateral Labor Agreement stated, that the Vietnamese government should implement the laws, regulations, and make the necessary the institutional reforms, to facilitate the automatic registration of independent labor unions in different industries. We request that the U.S. Congress and American diplomats in Vietnam, provide strong support to the Viet Labor Federation, by working closely with its members, and send clear messages to Vietnam asking officials, not to subject the independent labor unions to government denial or harassment, and secondly, to encourage training for technical assistance from international labor organizations, including the AFL-CIO, for all labor unions in Vietnam. Thank you.